501 Riddles and Trivia Questions:

For Teachers of Kids (7-13)

Jackie Bolen +

Jennifer Booker Smith

Table of Contents

About the Author: Jackie Bolen...........5
About the Author: Jennifer Booker Smith...........6
How to Use this Book...........7
Science...........8
    Easy 1 (9 questions)...........8
    Easy 2 (9 questions)...........9
    Medium (9 questions)...........10
    Difficult (9 questions)...........11
Animals...........12
    Easy 1 (8 questions)...........12
    Easy 2 (8 questions)...........13
    Easy 3 (8 questions)...........13
    Medium 1 (9 questions)...........14
    Medium 2 (7 questions)...........15
    Medium 3 (7 questions)...........15
    Difficult (7 questions)...........16
Math...........17
    Easy 1 (8 questions)...........17
    Easy 2 (8 questions)...........18
    Medium (8 questions)...........19
    Difficult 1 (9 questions)...........20
    Difficult 2 (9 questions)...........21
Geography...........22
    Easy 1 (8 questions)...........22
    Easy 2 (8 questions)...........22
    Medium (9 questions)...........23
    Difficult (9 questions)...........24
Countries Around the World...........25
    Easy 1 (8 questions)...........25
    Easy 2 (8 questions)...........26
    Medium (8 questions)...........26
    Difficult 1 (8 questions)...........27
    Difficult 2 (8 questions)...........28
The Human Body...........29
    Easy (8 questions)...........29
    Medium (8 questions)...........29
    Difficult (7 questions)...........30
Language...........31
    Easy (8 questions)...........31
    Easy 2 (8 questions)...........32
    Medium (9 questions)...........32
    Difficult 1 (8 questions)...........33

- Difficult 2 (7 questions) 34
- Finish that Sentence 35
  - #1 (6 questions) 35
  - #2 (7 questions) 35
  - #3 (7 questions) 36
- Holidays and Special Days 37
  - Easy (8 questions) 37
  - Medium/ Difficult (7 questions) 38
- Food 39
  - Easy 1 (8 questions) 39
  - Easy 2 (7 questions) 40
  - Easy 3 (7 questions) 40
  - Medium (8 questions) 41
  - Difficult (8 questions) 42
- Books/ Movies/ Pop-Culture 43
  - Easy (9 questions) 43
  - Medium (9 questions) 44
  - Difficult (9 questions) 45
- People 46
  - Easy (8 questions) 46
  - Difficult (9 questions) 47
- Sports 48
  - Easy (9 questions) 48
  - Medium (9 questions) 49
  - Difficult (9 questions) 50
- General Knowledge 51
  - Easy 1 (9 questions) 51
  - Easy 2 (9 questions) 52
  - Medium (8 questions) 53
  - Difficult (8 questions) 54
- Riddles 55
  - Easy 1 (5 riddles) 55
  - Easy 2 (5 riddles) 55
  - Easy 3 (5 riddles) 56
  - Easy 4 (4 riddles) 56
  - Easy 5 (4 riddles) 57
  - Medium 1 (5 riddles) 57
  - Medium 2 (5 riddles) 58
  - Difficult 1 (5 riddles) 58
  - Difficult 2 (5 riddles) 59
  - Difficult 3 (5 riddles) 59
  - Difficult 4 (6 riddles) 60
- Before You Go 60

Copyright 2015 by Jackie Bolen + Jennifer Booker Smith

All rights reserved. No part of this publication may be reproduced, distributed, or transmitted in any form or by any means, including photocopying, recording or other electronic or mechanical means without the prior written permission of the publisher, except in the case of brief quotations in critical reviews and certain other noncommercial uses permitted by copyright law. For permission requests, write to the publisher/ author at the address below.

Jackie Bolen: wealthyenglishteacher@gmail.com

About the Author: Jackie Bolen

I've been teaching English in South Korea for a decade to every level and type of student and I've taught every age from kindergarten kids to adults. Most of my time has centered around teaching at two universities: five years at a science and engineering school out in the rice paddies of Chungcheongnam-Do, and four years at a major university in Busan where I now teach high level classes for students majoring in English. In my spare time, you can usually find me outside surfing, biking, hiking or on the hunt for the most delicious kimchi I can find.

In case you were wondering what my academic qualifications are, I hold a Master of Arts in Psychology. During my time in Korea I've successfully completed both the Cambridge CELTA and DELTA teaching certification programs. I truly hope that you find this book useful and would love it if you sent me an email with any questions or feedback that you might have —I'll always take the time to personally respond (wealthyenglishteacher@gmail.com).

Jackie Bolen Around the Internet

ESL Speaking (www.eslspeaking.org)

Jackie Bolen (www.jackiebolen.com)

Twitter: @bolen_jackie

About the Author: Jennifer Booker Smith

I have a Master of Education in TESOL and have spent fifteen years teaching students of all ages in Korea, from two-year-old preschoolers barely out of diapers to businessmen and even a semester as a teacher trainer at an education university. However, my greatest love is the middle primary grades—I left a fairly cushy teacher trainer position to return to the elementary classroom. In that age group, I've taught all ability levels from false beginner to near-native returnees.

When I'm not teaching, like Jackie, you can often find me hiking. I've taken up running recently and will soon be running my third half marathon. Teaching takes up a lot more "free" time than non-teachers will ever realise, so it's important to recharge the batteries and being outside is my favourite way to do just that.

You can get in touch with me by emailing jenniferteacher@gmail.com. I'd love to hear from you and help you with your classes in any way that I can, particularly if you have a difficult children's class and would like some advice about that. I'll do my best to assist you.

How to Use this Book

If you teach elementary school children, 501 Riddles and Trivia Questions: For Teachers of Kids (7-13) will make the perfect addition to your personal library. There are a few different ways you can use the trivia and riddles, including:

Warm-Up: Start your classes off with a few brain-teasers to get your students active and ready for the main lesson. Each section (7-10 trivia questions, or 4-6 riddles) should take less than five minutes to complete. Be sure to keep track at the bottom of each section the date and class you used them in. **Hint**: Use pencil and you can erase it at the end of the school year.

Time-Filler: Keep this book handy to pull out in case you have a few extra minutes at the end of the lesson. It's the perfect way to fill some dead-time and you can choose a section relevant to whatever you're teaching (science/ math/ language, etc.). Again, keep track of the date and class in pencil at the bottom of each page.

Early-Finisher Activity: You know those annoying students who always seem to finish everything really quickly? Print off a stack of these trivia and riddles worksheets and let students get to work. Make sure you follow the links to get the PDF worksheets, minus the answers!

Web-Quest: If you're teaching your students how to find information on the Internet, the trivia question handouts will work perfectly. Each set of questions should take students between 1-2 minutes/ question, so a total of 7-15 minutes.

Science

For printable PDF worksheets of this section, please go to: www.eslspeaking.org/science.

Easy 1 (9 questions)

What color do you get when you mix red and blue? (Purple)

What color do you get when you mix blue and yellow? (Green)

Does the Earth move around the sun, or does the sun move around the Earth? (The Earth moves around the sun.)

What two things can we see in the sky usually only at night? (The moon and stars)

How many sides does a cube have? (Six)

What is the name for the moon when it is the biggest? (Full moon)

At what temperature does water freeze? (O degrees Celsius, 32 degrees Fahrenheit)

If you freeze water, what is it called? (Ice)

How long does it take the Earth to make one complete rotation? (24 hours/ one day)

Easy 2 (9 questions)

What color do you get when you mix red and yellow? (Orange)

What color do you get when you mix red and white? (Pink)

Does ice sink or float in water? (It floats.)

At what temperature does water boil at? (100 degrees Celsius, 212 degrees Fahrenheit)

How many sides does a snowflake have? (Six)

Is the sun a star or planet? (A star)

What prevents you from floating away into space? (Gravity)

How many arms does a starfish have? (Five)

What is the most common plant on Earth? (Grass)

Medium (9 questions)

During a storm, can you see lightning, or hear thunder first? (See lightning)

How many planets are there? (Eight: Mercury, Venus, Earth, Mars, Jupiter, Saturn, Uranus, Neptune)

Which planet is closest to the sun? (Mercury)

Water is made up of which two things? (Hydrogen and oxygen)

Fire needs two things to live. What are they? (Fuel: gas/ paper/ wood, etc. and oxygen)

Plants need something in the air in order to grow. What is it? (Carbon dioxide)

Is an iguana a reptile, amphibian or mammal? (A reptile)

Which planet is closest to the Earth? (Venus)

What is the common name for NaCl? Hint: It's something we often put into food. (Salt)

Difficult (9 questions)

What are the eight planets? (Mercury, Venus, Earth, Mars, Jupiter, Saturn, Uranus, Neptune)

What is the hottest planet in our solar system? (Venus)

Why can you see lightning before you can hear thunder? (Light travels faster than sound.)

Humans and animals need something in the air in order to live. What is it? (Oxygen)

At what point does the temperature on the Fahrenheit and Celsius scales meet? (-40 degrees)

What is the deepest point in the ocean? (Mariana Trench)

What gas, released by a car, stops your blood from carrying oxygen? (Carbon Monoxide)

What do you call someone who studies plants? (Botanist)

Who developed the theory of evolution? (Charles Darwin)

Animals

For printable PDF worksheets of this section, please go to: www.eslspeaking.org/animals.

Easy 1 (8 questions)

Which animal hops and has a pouch where they keep their babies? (Kangaroo)

What is the biggest animal? (Blue Whale)

What is the tallest animal? (Giraffe)

Which animal eats only bamboo? (Giant Panda)

True or False. There are tigers in Africa. (False)

How many legs does a spider have? (Eight)

What is the fastest animal in the world? (Cheetah)

How many arms does an octopus have? (Eight)

Easy 2 (8 questions)

What is a baby dog called? (Puppy)

Which animal sleeps most of the winter? (Bear)

In which country are you most likely to find a kangaroo? (Australia)

What is a group of lions called? (Pride)

What is the only continent on earth where giraffes live in the wild (outside of zoos)? (Africa)

How many legs does a butterfly have? (Six)

A 'doe' is what kind of animal? (Female deer)

True or false? Bats are mammals. (True, they give birth to live young and feed them milk.)

Easy 3 (8 questions)

What is a baby cat called? (Kitten)

What is the largest bird? (Ostrich)

Where do giant pandas live? (China)

What is the lightest bird in the world? (Hummingbird)

What kind of pattern does a zebra have? (Stripes)

What kind of pattern does a leopard have? (Spots)

What is the largest animal on land? (African elephant)

Name a land animal that has no legs. (Snake)

Medium 1 (9 questions)

Sharks have no bones. What do they have instead? (Cartilage)

True or false? Mice can live for 10 years. (False. Wild mice live up to one year and pet mice up to two.)

What is the largest type of 'big cat' in the world? (Tiger)

What part of their bodies do crocodiles use to release heat? (Mouth—they have no sweat glands).

Are butterflies insects? (Yes, they have three body sections and six legs, like all insects.)

What are female elephants called? (Cows)

What are male elephants called? (Bulls)

Bees are found on every continent of earth except for one; which is it? (Antarctica)

Which animal makes a disgusting smell if it sprays you? (Skunk)

Medium 2 (7 questions)

What is a bee home called? (Hive)

What is the biggest shark? (Great White Shark)

What is a group of birds called? (Flock)

What is the name of an adult female horse? (Mare)

What are baby goats called? (Kids)

True or false? Rabbits are born blind. (True)

What is a baby seal called? (Pup)

Medium 3 (7 questions)

What is the study of birds called? (Ornithology)

How many legs does a crab have? (10)

How many toes does a dog have? (18)

What kind of bear can you find in Canada and the USA that is extremely dangerous? (Grizzly Bear)

True or false? Cats spend about 15 hours a day sleeping. (True, but some breeds sleep even more.)

True or false? Cougars are herbivores. (False. All cats are carnivores, or meat eaters.)

What is a baby bear called? (Cub)

Difficult (7 questions)

What is the word for a big fear of spiders? (Arachnophobia)

Name one big cat which <u>doesn't</u> roar. (Cheetah, cougar/ mountain lion/ puma/ panther, snow + clouded leopard).

What kind of animal is a dolphin? (Mammal)

What is the largest primate in the world? (Eastern Gorilla)

True or false? Owls are far-sighted, meaning that anything within a few inches/ centimeters of their eyes can't be seen properly. (True)

What is the deadliest snake in the world? (Black Mamba)

What is the largest penguin? (Emperor penguin)

Math

For printable PDF worksheets of this section, please go to: www.eslspeaking.org/math.

Easy 1 (8 questions)

If you're in the USA, how many pennies equals $2? (200)

In the USA, how many quarters equals $1? (Four)

In the USA, how many dimes equals $3? (30)

I had $10 and went shopping. I bought each member of my family: brother, sister, father, mother and myself an ice cream for $1 each. How much money do I have left? ($5)

Does sum mean add or subtract? (Add)

How many sides does a triangle have? (Three)

How many sides does a square have? (Four)

If I use a $5 bill to pay for something that is $2.79, how much change should I get? ($2.21)

Easy 2 (8 questions)

How many zeroes are in the number one hundred thousand? (Five)

John's dad bought 21 apples at the store. John wants to eat them all in one week. How many should he eat each day? (Three)

It is 10:15, but Tom feels hungry and asks his teacher when lunch is. At 12:00, she says. How long does Tom have to wait? (1 hour, 45 minutes)

How many hours are there in three days? (72 hours)

How many minutes are there in 5 hours? (300 minutes)

Which number is next? 0, 2, 5, 9 (14, +5. Increase the number you add by one.)

Which number is next? 1, 20, 300, 4,000, 50,000 (600,000. Add one to the first number and a zero to the end.)

If I use a $20 bill to pay for something that is $11.46, how much change should I get? ($8.54)

Medium (8 questions)

There are seven tables. Six tables have ten people, but one table has eight people. How many people are there? (68 people)

Hundreds, thousands, millions, billions, what is next? (Trillions)

What is 0.45 as a percentage? (45%)

Take the numbers 0 to 9. Add them together. What number do you have? (45)

What is 160 divided by 5? (32)

What is 50% of 250? (125)

What is 30% of 20? (Six)

How many hours are there in 1 week? (168 hours)

I bought two things costing $4.21 and $8.34 with $20. How much change would I get? ($7.45)

Difficult 1 (9 questions)

What do you call an object with five sides? (Pentagon)

What do you call an object with six sides? (Hexagon)

How many zeroes are in the number one hundred twenty-six thousand? (Three)

How many zeroes are in the number nine hundred and eight thousand, five hundred and forty (2)

How many degrees do the angles in a square have? (90 degrees)

How many degrees do the angles in an equal-sided triangle have? (120 degrees)

As a percentage, what is 11/20? (55%)

As a percentage, what is 39/200? (19.5%)

I bought three things at the store costing $1.44, $2.99 and $2.21. Tax is an extra 10%. How much will it cost? ($7.30)

Difficult 2 (9 questions)

As a percentage, what is 37/300? (12.3%)

An empty bus pulls up to a stop and 10 people get on. At the next stop five people get off and twice as many people get on as at the first stop. At the third stop, 25 get off. How many people are on the bus? (One: the driver)

In gym class, Jen has to run around the track 15 times. Each lap is 400 m. How many kilometers does she run? (Six kilometers)

In kilometers, what is 10,500 meters? (10.5 kilometers)

How many meters is 850 centimeters? (8.5 meters)

As a fraction, what does 75% equal? (¾, three fourths)

As a fraction, what does 66.6% equal? (□ , two thirds)

How many minutes are there in one day? (1440 minutes)

I bought four things at the store costing $1.24, $2.21, $3, and $4.21. Will $10 be enough? (No, it will cost $10.66)

Geography

For printable PDF worksheets of this section, please go to: www.eslspeaking.org/geography.

Easy 1 (8 questions)

What is the longest river in the world? (Nile)

What is the tallest mountain in the world? (Mount Everest)

What is the name of the highest mountain in Africa? (Mount Kilimanjaro, located in Tanzania)

In which country can you find the Great Barrier Reef? (Australia)

Does latitude run North to South, or East to West? (East to West)

What is the largest continent? (Asia)

In which ocean can I find Hawaii? (Pacific Ocean)

Where can I find the most famous pyramids in the world? (Egypt)

Easy 2 (8 questions)

On which continent can I find the Alps mountain range? (Europe)

What is the smallest continent? (Australia)

On which continent can I find the Rocky Mountains? (North America)

Which ocean can I find to the East of Canada? (Atlantic Ocean)

Which ocean can I find to the West of the USA? (Pacific Ocean)

In terms of size, what is the biggest state in the USA? (Alaska)

Which country is bigger in size: Canada or the USA? (Canada)

What is the biggest ocean on Earth? (Pacific Ocean)

Medium (9 questions)

Which US state is known as the Aloha State? (Hawaii)

San Antonio is a city in which American state? (Texas)

Which country has the tallest building in the world? (Dubai)

In which country can you find Machu Picchu? (Peru)

In which country can you find Angkor Wat? (Cambodia)

What line has a latitude of zero degrees? (The Equator)

Which continent has the most countries? (Africa with 54)

What is the point in Canada and USA where water flows West to the Pacific Ocean, and East to the Atlantic Ocean? (The Continental Divide)

What line has a longitude of zero degrees? (The Prime Meridian)

Difficult (9 questions)

What is the tallest mountain, if you consider above, and below the ocean? Hint: it's not Mount Everest or K2! (Mauna Kea. Most of its height is underwater.)

What is the world's largest lake? (Caspian Sea, Lake Superior is the largest freshwater lake.)

What is the world's deepest lake? (Lake Baikal)

What is the world's biggest river? (Amazon)

What is the world's driest place? (Atacama Desert in Chile)

What is the wettest place on Earth? (Mawsynram in north-east India)

Where was the highest temperature on Earth recorded? (Death Valley, California, USA)

What major city has the coldest average temperature? (Ulaanbaatar, Mongolia)

Name three countries that start with the letter "R." (Romania, Russia, Rwanda)

Countries Around the World

For printable PDF worksheets of this section, please go to: www.eslspeaking.org/countries.

Easy 1 (8 questions)

Which country is Paris the capital city of? (France)

Name three countries in North America (The USA, Canada, Mexico)

Which country is the biggest in terms of size? (Russia)

Which country has the most people? (China)

What is the name of the money in Canada? (Dollar)

Who was the first president of the USA? (George Washington)

What is the capital city of England? (London)

What is Canada's biggest city? (Toronto)

Easy 2 (8 questions)

In which city does the US president live? (Washington, D.C.)

What is the name of the American president's house? (The White House)

How many islands make up Japan? (Four)

In which country could I find the Leaning Tower of Pisa? (Italy)

Helsinki is the capital city of which country? (Finland)

Which continent has the most people? (Asia)

From which country does the company Sony come? (Japan)

From which country does the company Samsung come? (South Korea)

Medium (8 questions)

Kia is a car company based in which country? (South Korea)

What is the second biggest country? (Canada, Russia is first)

What is the capital city of Canada? (Ottawa)

What is the capital city of Ireland? (Dublin)

The USA received the Statue of Liberty as a gift from which country? (France)

On which continent can I find the Sahara desert? (Africa)

What is the currency of Denmark called? (The krone)

Which country has the second most people? (India, China is first)

Difficult 1 (8 questions)

Where does the leader of the Catholic Church, the Pope, live? (Vatican City)

What is the capital of Northern Ireland? (Belfast)

What is the capital city of Australia? (Canberra)

What is the capital city of New Zealand? (Wellington)

Which country has three capitals: Pretoria, Bloemfontein, and Cape Town? (South Africa)

What is the second largest French-speaking city in the world? (Montreal, Canada)

What language do people speak in Brazil? (Portuguese)

Korea is divided into North and South Korea. Which one is a friend of the USA? (South Korea)

Difficult 2 (8 questions)

What is the capital city of Bulgaria? (Sophia)

What is Easter Island famous for? (Massive stone statues)

What is the only US state to have one syllable? (Maine)

In which Canadian city can I find the Prime Minister? (Ottawa)

Which US state is known as the volunteer state? (Tennessee)

What Canadian province has the slogan, "Wild Rose Country?" (Alberta)

What are the four maritime provinces of Canada? (Newfoundland, New Brunswick, Nova Scotia, Prince Edward Island)

Where does the Prime Minister of Britain live? (10 Downing Street)

The Human Body

For printable PDF worksheets of this section, please go to: www.eslspeaking.org/humanbody.

Easy (8 questions)

What is between your leg and your foot? (Ankle)

What is between your arm and hand? (Wrist)

How many times does an adult blink in one minute? (An average of 10 times)

The left side of your brain controls which side of your body? (Right side)

What percent of a human is water? (About 70%)

What is the main purpose of your eyebrow? (To keep sweat out of your eyes)

Can you sneeze with your eyes open? (No, it's impossible.)

Do you burn more calories watching TV or sleeping? (Sleeping. Turn that TV off!)

Medium (8 questions)

In liters, how much blood does an average body have? (5.6 L)

When you blink, how many muscles do you use? (About 200)

At what age do you begin to shrink/ get shorter? (Age 30)

Which of the nails on your hand grows the most quickly? (The middle one)

What are the bones called that protect your heart? (Ribs)

What is the stage of sleep when you often dream? (REM sleep, REM = Rapid eye movement)

What carries oxygen through your blood? (Red blood cells)

Which are the blood vessels that carry blood to your heart called? How about the ones that take blood away? (Veins—to the heart, Arteries—away from the heart)

Difficult (7 questions)

What are the things on your tongue that taste things? (Taste buds)

What is the colored part of the eye called? (The iris)

What are the two holes in your nose called? (Nostrils)

How many bones does a human body have? (206)

Where is the smallest bone in your body found? (The middle ear—stapes or stirrup bone)

What do antibiotics fight? What do they not fight? (Bacteria, not viruses)

How many muscles do we use when we smile? (At least 36)

Language

For printable PDF worksheets of this section, please go to: www.eslspeaking.org/language.

Easy (8 questions)

What word that sounds the same can mean a letter in the alphabet, a drink, or something you use when you play golf? (T/ Tea/ Tee)

What word that sounds the same can mean correct, or to use a pen? (Right/ Write)

A cow is an animal. What is the special name for cow meat when you eat it? (Beef)

A pig is an animal. What is the special name for pig meat when you eat it? (Pork)

What is your mother's mother called? (Grandmother/ grandma)

What is a dried grape called? (Raisin)

What is a mountain that can erupt called? (Volcano)

What is another word for place you are going? (Destination)

Easy 2 (8 questions)

What can you buy at a butcher shop? (Meat)

What does ASAP stand for? (As soon as possible)

In what room of your house do you cook food? (Kitchen)

In what room of your house do you wash your hands and use the toilet? (Bathroom)

Who flies an airplane? (Pilot)

What is a baby frog called? (Tadpole)

What is a piece of ice floating in the ocean called? (Iceberg)

What is the name of the book with words and definitions? (Dictionary)

Medium (9 questions)

What does PC stand for? (Personal computer, or politically correct)

What word that sounds the same can mean a number, or someone that gets first place in a contest? (One/ Won)

What is your sister's husband called? (Brother-in-law)

What is your father's father's father called? (Your great-grandfather)

Stratus and nimbus are kinds of what? (Clouds)

Gale and breeze describe different speeds of what? (Wind)

What does carnivore mean? (Only eats meat)

What does herbivore mean? (Only eats plants)

How many vowels are there in English? (5: A/E/I/O/U, + sometimes Y)

Difficult 1 (8 questions)

Do you know any words with more than 8 letters? (Many answers possible)

What is the word for very, very hungry? (Ravenous/ famished/ starving)

This person races horses for a job. What is the job name? (Jockey)

What document do you need if you want to travel to another country? (Passport)

What is the name for a person or animal that eats both plants and meat? (Omnivore)

What is a dried plum called? (Prune)

What single word can be used with show, brief and stair to make new words? (Case: showcase, briefcase, staircase)

A palindrome is a word or phrase that is the same front to back, and back to front. Can you think of any? (Radar, race car, eye, etc.)

Difficult 2 (7 questions)

What is the job name for a person who studies rocks? (Geologist)

What does an entomologist study? (Insects)

What is used to measure temperature? (Thermometer)

If someone asks you to RSVP, what do you need to do? (Tell them if you're coming to the event or not)

Homonyms are words that sounds the same, but have different meanings and spelling. Can you think of any? (Many answers possible)

What are the six most common letters in the English language? (R, S, T, L, N, E)

What is the distance from the center of a circle to a point on the circle called? (Radius)

Finish that Sentence

For printable PDF worksheets of this section, please go to: www.eslspeaking.org/sentence.

#1 (6 questions)

Dealing with something unpleasant. "Bite the _____." (Bullet)

Family is most important. "Blood is thicker than _____." (Water)

To begin something new, especially a relationship. "Break the _____." (Ice)

When someone doesn't say anything. "Did the cat get your _____?" (Tongue)

To die. "Kick the _____." (Bucket)

Make an apology. "Eat humble _____." (Pie)

#2 (7 questions)

Quitting something quickly. "Going cold _____." (Turkey)

Do more than expected. "Go the whole nine _____." (Yards)

To relax. "Let your hair _____." (Down)

To be very happy. "Pleased as _____." (Punch)

To annoy. "Rub the _____ _____." (Wrong way)

A rule that everyone knows. "Rule of _____." (Thumb)

Rescued from a situation you don't want to be in. "Saved by the _____." (Bell)

#3 (7 questions)

Showing that someone isn't welcome. "Give the cold _____." (Shoulder)

You can endure difficult things. "That which does not kill us makes us _____." (Stronger)

A popular, but controversial issue or topic. "Hot _____." (Potato)

Asking someone what they're thinking. "A penny for your _____." (Thoughts)

To reveal your true self. " Show your true _____." (Colors)

Share a secret. "Spill the _____." (Beans)

Starting the day off in a bad mood. "Waking up on the wrong side of the _____." (Bed)

Holidays and Special Days

For printable PDF worksheets of this section, please go to: www.eslspeaking.org/holidays.

Easy (8 questions)

When is Valentine's Day? (February 14th)

When is Halloween? (October 31st)

What kind of meat is traditionally eaten at Thanksgiving in Canada and the US? (Turkey)

An animal often brings colored eggs on this day. Which holiday and which animal? (Easter; A rabbit)

What is the holiday where children dress-up in costumes? (Halloween)

Which animals pull a sled for Santa? (Reindeer)

Who is the special Christmas animal with a red nose? (Rudolph the red-nosed reindeer)

People often play tricks on other people on this day. When is it? What is the holiday called? (April 1st, April Fool's Day)

Medium/ Difficult (7 questions)

Santa Claus rides in a special thing. What is it called? (A sled/ sleigh)

What is the holiday where parents often let children stay up past their bedtime? (December 31st—New Year's Eve)

People often wear green clothes on this holiday. What is it? Which month? (Saint Patrick's Day—March)

In the US, George Washington's birthday is a holiday, but in other English-speaking countries, a woman's birthday is celebrated. Who is she? (Queen Elizabeth)

What is the day after Christmas called in Canada, the UK, Ireland, Australia, and New Zealand? (Boxing Day)

During this holiday, you can't eat or drink from sunrise to sunset. What is it called? (Ramadan)

What is the Korean thanksgiving festival called? (Chu-seok)

Food

For printable PDF worksheets of this section, please go to: www.eslspeaking.org/food.

Easy 1 (8 questions)

Which animal does milk come from? (Cow)

What is the yellow part of an egg called? (Yolk)

What is the white, inside part of an egg called? (The white/ albumin)

What sweet food is made by bees? (Honey)

What is butter and cheese made from? (Milk)

What vegetable can you often see at Halloween outside of people's houses in the USA or Canada? (Pumpkins)

What is the main ingredient in ketchup? (Tomato)

What is the most popular fast food restaurant in the world? (McDonald's)

Easy 2 (7 questions)

Which country has the most McDonald's restaurants? (USA—almost 19,000)

Where do carrots, beets and radishes grow? (Under the ground)

Name two kinds of fruit that grow in bunches. (Bananas and grapes)

Which fruit is very bitter and yellow? (Lemon)

Which fruit is wine made from? (Grapes)

Are tomatoes fruit or vegetables? (Fruit)

Which vegetable are dill pickles made from? (Cucumbers)

Easy 3 (7 questions)

What color is an eggplant? (Purple)

Is a pumpkin a fruit or vegetable? (Fruit)

What is the first fruit that babies usually eat? (Banana, because it's easy to digest)

Which fruit skin is very slippery if you step on it while walking? (Banana)

Which cool and refreshing fruit contains 92% water? (Watermelon)

Which vegetable is yellow and has ears? (Corn)

Its color is the same as its name. Which fruit is it? (Orange)

Medium (8 questions)

What is the ingredient in bread that makes it rise? (Yeast)

This red fruit has seeds on the outside. (Strawberry)

What country does the rice dish "paella" come from? (Spain)

What is another name for the popular vegetable maize? (Corn)

What are three ways that you can cook an egg? (Scrambled, boiled, fried, poached, over-easy, sunny-side up, devilled, etc.)

What are four ways that you can eat a potato? (Mashed, salad, french fries, potato chips, scalloped, pan-fried, hashbrowns, etc.)

What is the main ingredient in guacamole? (Avocado)

What is the natural color of Coca-Cola if you don't include the artificial colors? (Green)

Difficult (8 questions)

Bangers and mash is a popular food in England. What is it? (Sausage and mashed potatoes)

This fruit is brown on the outside and white on the inside. If it falls off the tree, watch out! What is it? (Coconut)

Which vegetable is sauerkraut made from? (Cabbage)

How many small black seeds does an average strawberry have? (200)

How many apples does the average apple tree produce in one year? (400)

What is the very large, smelly fruit that you can find in many Asian countries? (Durian)

Which fruit was once known as a Chinese gooseberry? (Kiwi)

Which fruit or vegetable has the highest fat content? (Avocado)

Books/ Movies/ Pop-Culture

For printable PDF worksheets of this section, please go to: www.eslspeaking.org/books.

Easy (9 questions)

Who met three bears in the woods, after eating their food and taking a nap at their house? (Goldilocks)

Who is Peter Pan's magic friend? (Tinkerbell)

Who is Winnie-the-Pooh's tiger friend? (Tigger)

Which Dr. Seuss character hates Christmas? (The Grinch)

Which movie stars Woody and Buzz Lightyear? (Toy Story)

Which Disney princess was not born a human? (Ariel)

What is the name of Shrek's wife? (Fiona)

What is the name of the hero in *The Lion King*? (Simba)

What kind of dogs was Cruella de Vil's favorite? (Dalmations)

Medium (9 questions)

In which city can you find Batman? (Gotham City)

What is Batman's real name? (Bruce Wayne)

What newspaper does Superman work for? (The Daily Planet)

Babe is a famous animal that stars in a movie. What kind of animal is she? (Pig)

What is Popeye's favourite vegetable? (Spinach)

Where do the Flintstones live? (Bedrock)

What is Fred Flintstone's favorite sport? (Bowling)

Which little boy was made by Gepetto? (Pinocchio)

Who is Homer Simpson's boss? (Mr. Burns)

Difficult (9 questions)

What does *Hakuna Matata* mean? (It is Swahili for "No worries.")

Wolverine is part of which group of superheroes? (The X-Men)

What was the name of Harry Potter's owl? (Hedwig)

Who sang *Hakuna Matata* in *The Lion King*? (Timon, the meerkat, and Pumbaa, the warthog)

What is the name of the vehicle in which Scooby Doo and his friends travel? (The Mystery Machine)

Which two Disney princesses are archers? (Merida and Mulan)

Which Disney princess is based on a real person? (Pocahontas; Mulan is based on a legend, and may or may not have been real.)

What is the name of the Kung Fu Panda in the film with the same name? (Po)

Where can you catch the Hogwart's train? (Platform nine and three quarters at Kings Cross)

People

For printable PDF worksheets of this section, please go to: www.eslspeaking.org/people.

Easy (8 questions)

What is the first name of the man who started the Ford car company? (Henry)

Who is the founder of Microsoft? (Bill Gates)

Who was the leader of Germany during World War Two? (Adolf Hitler)

Who was the founder of Apple? (Steve Jobs)

Who was the first person to walk on the moon? (Neil Armstrong)

In the original Jackson family, how many singing children were there? (Five)

Who is the famous South African that fought for equal rights for white and black people? (Nelson Mandela)

Who wrote Harry Potter? (J.K. Rowling)

Difficult (9 questions)

Who is the current vice-president of the USA? (Joe Biden)

What is the name of the most recent US president to be killed while serving as president? (John F. Kennedy)

Who was the British prime minister during World War Two? (Winston Churchill)

There is a women from Macedonia who is famous for helping poor people in India. What is her name? (Mother Theresa)

Who is the political and spiritual leader of Tibet? (The Dalai Lama)

Who made January 1st as the start of the year? (Julius Caesar, when he created the Julian calendar)

Who was the British Prime Minister during the 1980's? (Margaret Thatcher)

In Romeo and Juliet, how did Romeo die? (Poison)

Who invented the telephone? (Alexander Graham Bell)

Sports

For printable PDF worksheets of this section, please go to: www.eslspeaking.org/sports.

Easy (9 questions)

Michael Jordan is a famous sports player. What sport did he play? (Basketball, and baseball, briefly)

Wayne Gretzky is a famous sports player. What sport did he play? Bonus: What was the first team he played for? (Ice Hockey; The Edmonton Oilers)

Joe Montana is a famous sports player. What sport did he play? Bonus: Which team did he play for? (American football; San Francisco 49'ers)

Tony Hawk is professional athlete. What sport does he do? (Skateboarding)

What is the name of the most famous cycling competition in the world? (Tour de France)

There are two American sisters who are famous tennis players. What are their names? (Venus and Serena Williams)

In American football, which player throws the ball? (Quarterback)

Name a team sport that doesn't use a ball. (Hockey; it uses a puck)

How often are the Olympics held? (Every 2 years; alternating summer and winter)

Medium (9 questions)

Which major tennis tournament is played on a grass court? (Wimbledon)

Which major tennis tournament is played on a clay court? (The French Open)

What is the sport where you throw "stones/ rocks" into a "house?" (Curling)

In which sport can you have a knuckleball or a curveball? (Baseball; they are kinds of pitches.)

What is the name of the American cyclist who won the Tour De France many times? (Lance Armstrong)

What are the three sports in a triathlon and what order are they in? (Swimming, biking, then running)

Which sport did Babe Ruth play? Bonus: Which record did he break? (Baseball; most home-runs)

How long is a full marathon? (26 miles/ 42 kilometers)

Name three pieces of equipment used to play badminton. (Net, racket, shuttlecock/ birdie)

Difficult (9 questions)

What are the four major tennis tournaments? (The US Open, Australian Open, French Open and Wimbledon)

Where will the 2020 Olympics be held? (Tokyo, Japan)

What does NHL stand for? (National Hockey League)

What does CFL stand for? Hint: It's a sport's league. (Canadian Football League)

In golf, what is it called when you use the recommended number of shots? (Par)

In golf, what is it called when you use one more shot than par? How about one less than par? (Bogey; birdie)

How many Olympic medals did American swimmer Michael Phelps win before he retired? (22, in three Olympics)

In snooker, what is the color of the last ball you have to sink? (Black)

What is the name of the sport where you ride quickly down an ice track at high speed? (Bobsled or luge)

General Knowledge

For printable PDF worksheets of this section, please go to: www.eslspeaking.org/general.

Easy 1 (9 questions)

What company makes the iPod? (Apple)

When did World War Two start and end? (1939-1945)

In the Christian religion, what is the most important book? (The Bible)

In the Bible, who were the first man and woman? (Adam and Eve)

In billions, how many people are there on the Earth today? (Just over 7 billion)

How many days does March have? (31)

How many days does September have? (30)

Ancient history is referred to as "B.C." For example, 156 B.C. What does B.C. stand for? (Before Christ)

In music, what does "forte" mean? (Loud)

Easy 2 (9 questions)

What is the seventh month? (July)

What is the most common hair color in the world? (Black)

In a normal year, how many days does February have? (28)

What is the most common language spoken? (Mandarin—15% of all people in the world)

How much of the Earth is covered with water? (About ☐ , or 66%)

How many states are there in the USA? (50)

Does salt cause ice to melt more slowly, or more quickly? (More quickly)

In minutes, how long does it take the average person to fall asleep? (Seven minutes)

In music, what does "allegro" mean? (Fast/ brisk tempo)

Medium (8 questions)

What is the name of the system of temperature used in the USA? (Fahrenheit)

What is the second most common language spoken in the world? (Spanish—6% of all people in the world)

What do the opposite sides of a die add up to? (Seven)

In Canada, the leader is not called the president. What is his or her title? (Prime Minister)

In the Muslim religion, what is the most important book? (The Koran)

What are three others ways you can say zero? (Nada, zip, zilch, nought, naught)

On which street can you find the New York Stock Exchange? (Wall Street)

What does a composer do? (Write music)

Difficult (8 questions)

How often is a leap year? (Once every four years; February 29th is Leap Day.)

Who is the current head of the Catholic Church? (Pope Francis)

How many dots are there on a pair of dice? (42)

What is the minimum age you have to be to sign up for Facebook? (13)

Which number under fifty has all the letters of its name in alphabetical order? (Forty)

What do some people search for at the end of a rainbow? (Pot of gold)

In thousands, how many languages are spoken in the world today? (About 6000)

A.D. does not stand for "After Death." What does it mean? (Anno Domini—Latin, for "In the year of the Lord.")

Riddles

For printable PDF worksheets of this section, please go to: www.eslspeaking.org/riddles.

Easy 1 (5 riddles)

What is once in a minute, twice in a moment, but never in a thousand years? (The Letter M)

Some people think I go too slow. Others think I go too fast. Most people are always checking me. What am I? (Time)

What is something that gets wetter as it dries? (Towel)

I start and end with the letter E. I contain only one letter besides E. What am I? (Eye)

What can you catch, but not throw? (A cold)

Easy 2 (5 riddles)

What is full of holes but can still hold water? (Sponge)

What food has no beginning, no middle and no end? (Donut)

How much dirt is there in a hole that is 3.45 m by 6.21 m? Hint: You don't need a calculator. (None—it's a hole!)

If you have one, you want to share it. If you share it, you haven't got it. What is it? (Secret)

I have legs but I can't walk. A strong back but I don't do work. Two arms but I can't move them. What am I? (Armchair)

Easy 3 (5 riddles)

I have no lungs, but I can breathe. I have no life, but I live and die. I have no legs, but I can dance. What am I? (Fire)

What has a face and two hands, but no arms and legs? (Clock)

What goes up but never goes back down? (Age)

What goes down but never goes back up? (Rain)

You have something that other people use far more often than you. What is it? (Your name)

Easy 4 (4 riddles)

What is biggest when new but gets smaller with use? (Many answers: soap, pencil, etc.)

What do you have to break before you can use it? (Egg)

What goes up when rain comes down? (Umbrella)

What has a head, a foot, and four legs? (Bed)

Easy 5 (4 riddles)

I sometimes run, but I cannot walk. You always follow me around. What am I? (Your nose)

If you cut me, I won't cry, but you will! What am I? (Onion)

I have many eyes, but I cannot see. What am I? (Potato)

I have more stories than any other building. What am I? (Library)

Medium 1 (5 riddles)

What has four fingers and a thumb but isn't living? (Glove)

I am a man, but I'll never have a wife. Water gives me life, but the sun brings death. What am I? (Snowman)

What are two things you can never eat for breakfast? (Lunch and dinner)

Tom was out for a walk. It started to rain but he didn't have a jacket, hat or umbrella. However, not a single hair on his head got wet? How? (He's bald!)

This is an ancient invention still used today that allows people to see through walls. (Window or glass)

Medium 2 (5 riddles)

During what month do people sleep the least? (February—it has the fewest days)

A man has six sons. Each son has a sister. How many children does the man have? (Seven: six boys and one girl)

I start with a *P* and end with an *E* and have thousands of letters. What am I? (Post Office)

I am always coming, but I never arrive today. What am I? (Tomorrow)

I can't speak, but I always tell the truth. What am I? (Mirror)

Difficult 1 (5 riddles)

On a nice, sunny day a ship suddenly began to sink. There was nothing wrong with the ship. Why did it sink? (It's a submarine.)

What has many keys but that can't open any doors? (Piano)

The sun can bake them. Your hand can pick them. Your mouth can taste them. Your feet can walk on them. What are they? (Grapes)

What loses its head in the morning, but gets it back at night? (Pillow)

It has been around for millions of years, but it's never more than a month old. What is it? (Moon)

Difficult 2 (5 riddles)

How many seconds are there in a year? Hint-you don't need a calculator and the number is less than 100. (24: each month has a 2nd and 22nd day)

A cat has one, a horse two, an elephant three. What am I? (Vowels: A, E, I, O, U)

Dead people eat me all the time. Living people will die if they eat me. What am I? (Nothing)

I'm in the air, but I'm not always there. I can be felt or held. It's easier to see me if you live in a cold place. What am I? (Your breath)

Who has married many people but has never been married? (Priest)

Difficult 3 (5 riddles)

Give me food and I grow. Give me water and I die. What am I? (Fire)

I am the most slippery country in the world. What am I? (Greece-Grease!)

I visit you every night but am lost every day. What am I? (Stars/ Moon)

I am the same from front to back and back to front, and you can drive me very fast. What am I? (Race car)

I am not alive, but I can die. What am I? (Battery)

Difficult 4 (6 riddles)

A 20-year-old man has had only five birthdays. How is that possible? (He was born on February 29th, Leap Year Day)

I can travel around the world without leaving the corner? What am I? (Stamp)

I never ask questions, but am often answered. What am I? (Phone or doorbell)

I am read the same forward, backward, and upside down. What am I? (SWIMS, SOS)

How can you add eight eights and get 1,000? (888+88+8+8+8=1,000)

You throw away the outside before you eat me and throw away the inside after you eat me. What am I? (Corn on the cob)

Before You Go

If you found 501 Riddles and Trivia Questions: For Teachers of Kids (7-13) useful, please head on over to Amazon and leave a review. It will help other teachers like you find the book. Also be sure to check out our other books on Amazon at www.amazon.com/author/jackiebolen.

Printed by Amazon Italia Logistica S.r.l.
Torrazza Piemonte (TO), Italy

54313857R00036